HISTORY MAKERS
PAST AND PRESENT

Ruth Bader Ginsburg

Joy Gregory

AV2

www.openlightbox.com

AV2

Step 1
Go to www.openlightbox.com

Step 2
Enter this unique code
KXZGDUPBC

Step 3
Explore your interactive eBook!

CONTENTS
4 Who Was Ruth Bader Ginsburg?
6 Growing Up
8 Practice Makes Perfect
10 Key Events
12 What Is a Supreme Court Justice?
14 Influences
16 Overcoming Obstacles
18 Achievements and Successes
20 Write a Biography
22 Ruth Bader Ginsburg Timeline

AV2 is optimized for use on any device

Your interactive eBook comes with...

Contents
Browse a live contents page to easily navigate through resources

Audio
Listen to sections of the book read aloud

Videos
Watch informative video clips

Weblinks
Gain additional information for research

Slideshows
View images and captions

Try This!
Complete activities and hands-on experiments

Key Words
Study vocabulary, and complete a matching word activity

Quizzes
Test your knowledge

Share
Share titles within your Learning Management System (LMS) or Library Circulation System

Citation
Create bibliographical references following the Chicago Manual of Style

This title is part of our AV2 digital subscription

1-Year K–5 Subscription
ISBN 978-1-7911-3320-7

Access hundreds of AV2 titles with our digital subscription.
Sign up for a FREE trial at www.openlightbox.com/trial

Ruth Bader Ginsburg

Contents

AV2 Book Code 2
Who Was Ruth Bader Ginsburg? 4
Growing Up 6
Practice Makes Perfect 8
Key Events 10
What Is a Supreme
Court Justice? 12
Influences 14
Overcoming Obstacles 16
Achievements and Successes 18
Write a Biography 20
Ruth Bader Ginsburg Timeline 22
Key Words/Index 23

History Makers: Past and Present

Who Was Ruth Bader Ginsburg?

Ruth Bader Ginsburg was a judge on the Supreme Court of the United States. Her formal title was **associate justice**. She was the second woman appointed to the court. Her term began in 1993 and lasted 27 years.

Ruth was a **feminist** trailblazer. She became a lawyer in 1959. Back then, few women had law degrees. As a young lawyer, she argued several cases before the Supreme Court. Some of these cases were about laws that treated women and men differently.

Besides being the Supreme Court's second female justice, Ruth was also the first Jewish woman to take on the role.

People were drawn to this tiny but fierce **jurist**. Over time, Ruth became a pop culture icon. Her face appeared on t-shirts. Quotes by her appeared on posters and coffee mugs. People copied the collars and **jabots** she wore with her judicial robes. Some people called her the "Notorious RBG." That playful nickname was similar to the stage name used by a well-known rap singer.

Ruth Bader Ginsburg 5

Growing Up

Joan Ruth Bader was born in Brooklyn, a **borough** of New York City, on March 15, 1933. She was the youngest of two daughters. Her older sister, Marilyn, died from illness at the age of six. At the time, Ruth was 14 months old.

Ruth was raised in a working-class neighborhood in Brooklyn. Her family was Jewish. Ruth's father, Nathan, was a **furrier**. Her mother, Celia, helped run the family business, while also taking care of the children. Times were tough for the Baders when Ruth was young. In the 1930s, the **Great Depression** took hold of the United States. Most people did not have the money to buy fur clothing.

Before Ruth was old enough to go to school, her family called her Joan, her given name. Her parents later learned that their daughter's school had several other students named Joan. To avoid confusion, they asked people to call their daughter Ruth. Family and friends also called her Kiki, a nickname her older sister had given her.

If it was not part of New York City, Brooklyn would be the fourth largest city in the United States. The borough is home to more than 2.7 million people.

History Makers: Past and Present

Map of the United States

LEGEND: New York | United States | Other Countries | Water | International Border | State Boundary

New York State Symbols

State Flag
Flag of New York

State Bird
Eastern Bluebird

State Flower
Rose

New York State FACTS

With more than **19.3 million people**, New York is the **fourth most populous U.S. state**, after California, Texas, and Florida.

Covering an area of **54,556 square miles** (141,300 sq. km), New York is the **27th largest state** in the country.

New York has more than **70,000 miles** (112,650 km) of **rivers and streams**.

Ruth Bader Ginsburg

Practice Makes Perfect

Ruth was a hard-working student. In 1946, she was the **valedictorian** at her eighth grade graduation. Ruth went on to attend Brooklyn's James Madison High School. It was during her high school years that she learned her mother had cancer. Celia Bader died in 1950, the day before her daughter graduated.

After high school, Ruth went on to study at Cornell University, in Ithaca, New York, where she had been accepted on a full **scholarship**. In 1954, Ruth graduated with a bachelor's degree in government. She earned top marks in all subjects.

Soon after her graduation, Ruth married Martin Ginsburg, whom she had met at Cornell. After a brief stint in Oklahoma, the couple moved to Cambridge, Massachusetts, in 1955. There, Martin studied at Harvard Law School. The following year, Ruth enrolled there as well. By this time, the couple's first child was 14 months old.

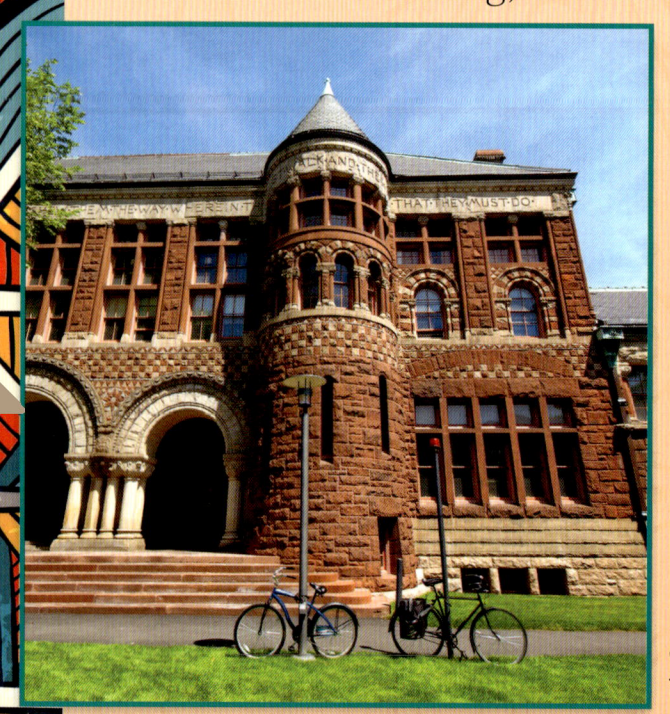

Founded in 1817, Harvard Law School consistently ranks as one of the top three law schools in the United States.

While they were both at Harvard, Martin was diagnosed with cancer. Ruth attended her own classes and helped Martin keep up with his classwork. During this time, she also cared for him and their daughter.

In 1958, the family moved to New York, where Martin, who was now in better health, began working for a law firm. Meanwhile, Ruth transferred to the city's Columbia Law School. She finished her last year of law school there, graduating in 1959. She and a male student tied for first place in the class.

RBG FACTS

Ruth and **Martin** had **two children**, Jane and James.

Ruth and **Martin** were **married** for **56 years** until he died in **2010**.

Ruth believed in **staying fit**. Even at the **age of 83**, she still did **20 push-ups** every day.

In 2011, Ruth returned to Harvard University to receive an honorary degree for her accomplishments in the legal field. She was one of nine people to receive honorary degrees that day.

Ruth Bader Ginsburg

Key Events

Shortly after graduating, Ruth found a job as a law clerk for a U.S. District Court judge. Her work involved researching laws and preparing reports for the judge. In 1963, she began teaching law at Rutgers University, in New Jersey.

In 1972, Columbia University hired Ruth to teach at its law school. She was the university's first female professor to get a teaching contract with **tenure**. During this time, Ruth also worked as **general counsel** for the American Civil Liberties Union (ACLU). The ACLU helps people who are not treated fairly in court.

Ruth worked on 34 cases that the ACLU took to the Supreme Court. Many involved laws that **discriminated** against women or men. She argued 6 of the 34 Supreme Court cases and won 5.

In 1980, President Jimmy Carter appointed Ruth to the U.S. Court of Appeals. Here, she reviewed rulings from lower courts to determine if the law had been applied properly.

Ruth's first successful Supreme Court case was in 1973. It determined that men married to military servicewomen should get the same benefits as women married to servicemen. Later, she won a case against a public university that did not allow women to take classes.

History Makers: Past and Present

Thoughts from RBG

People often asked Ruth what she thought about the law and society. They wanted to know her opinions about how women are treated. Her comments inspired women and men to work for change.

Ruth believed in a cooperative approach to solving problems.
"Fight for the things that you care about, but do it in a way that will lead others to join you."

Ruth stressed that women needed to have a role in society.
"Women belong in all places where decisions are being made."

The advice of Celia Bader stayed with her daughter throughout her life.
"My mother told me to be a lady. And for her, that meant be your own person, be independent."

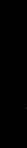

Staying composed was important to Ruth.
"When a thoughtless or unkind word is spoken, best tune out. Reacting in anger or annoyance will not advance one's ability to persuade."

Ruth talked about the impact being a lifelong reader had on her life.
"Reading is the key that opens doors to many good things in life. Reading shaped my dreams, and more reading helped me make my dreams come true."

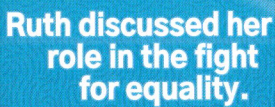

Ruth discussed her role in the fight for equality.
"I didn't change the **Constitution**; the equality principle was there from the start. I just was an advocate for seeing its full realization."

Ruth Bader Ginsburg

What Is a Supreme Court Justice?

A Supreme Court Justice is a judge on the U.S. Supreme Court. Every Supreme Court justice has training in the law. Most have worked as judges or lawyers in other courts for decades. Supreme Court justices are appointed for life, but they can retire.

The Supreme Court is based in Washington, DC. It is the highest court in the land. The court decides lawsuits between two or more states. It also hears cases about the U.S. Constitution. Court decisions are based on a majority of votes. To prevent tie votes, there is usually an uneven number of judges.

The court's decisions are final. Sometimes, a judge might disagree with the decision taken by the majority of judges. When this happens, the judge can describe why he or she disagrees with a written explanation known as dissent. If lawmakers agree with a dissent, they can write a new law.

How Are Judges Chosen?

The U.S. Congress sets the number of Supreme Court judges. Today's court has one chief justice and eight associates. When a Supreme Court judge dies or retires, the president nominates a replacement. The nominee meets with the Senate. This meeting, which can last for days, is called a senate hearing. At the hearing, senators ask the nominee legal and personal questions. They use that information to decide if the nominee would be a good Supreme Court Justice. The Senate can then accept or reject a nominee.

Supreme Court Judges 101

Sandra Day O'Connor
(1930–)

In 1981, Sandra Day O'Connor became the first woman appointed to the Supreme Court. She retired in 2006. Sandra grew up on a ranch in Arizona. She earned a law degree from Stanford University in 1952 but could not find a law firm that would hire a female lawyer. She found work with a county attorney instead. Sandra was a member of the Arizona State Senate from 1969 to 1974. Before joining the Supreme Court, she was a judge in Arizona.

Sonia Sotomayor
(1954–)

Sonia Sotomayor was appointed to the Supreme court in 2009. She is the third woman to be named to the U.S. Supreme Court and is also the first Hispanic woman on the court. Sonia was born in the Bronx, New York. Her parents were from Puerto Rico. Sonia graduated from Yale Law School in 1979. From 1979 to 1984, she worked as a **prosecutor**. Later, Sonia became a judge in the Southern District of New York. After that, she was a judge with the U.S. Court of Appeals until 2009.

Elena Kagan
(1960–)

Elena Kagan is the fourth woman to sit on the U.S. Supreme Court. She was born in New York City. Elena has degrees from Princeton and Oxford. She received her law degree from Harvard in 1986. Elena worked for a Supreme Court judge and a private law firm. Later, she taught law at the University of Chicago and Harvard University. In 2009, Elena became the first female **solicitor general** of the United States. She was appointed to the Supreme Court in 2010.

Amy Coney Barrett
(1972–)

The fifth woman appointed to the Supreme Court is Amy Coney Barrett. She was nominated in 2020 by President Donald Trump, about one week after Ruth Bader Ginsburg's death. Amy was born in New Orleans, Louisiana. She received her law degree from the University of Notre Dame in 1997. She later joined a private law firm, but returned to Notre Dame in 2002 to teach law. From 2017 to 2020, she served as a federal Court of Appeals judge.

Ruth Bader Ginsburg

Influences

Vladimir Nabokov

Two men influenced Ruth's legal career. She met both of them at Cornell University. Vladimir Nabokov taught literature at Cornell from 1948 to 1959. A celebrated writer, Vladimir was born in Russia, but became a U.S. citizen in 1945. At Cornell, he taught students about the power of language. Vladimir inspired Ruth to improve her writing and speaking skills. This would later help her to compose legal arguments.

Cornell University is made up of 16 different colleges and schools. The university has a total enrollment of more than 23,000 students.

Ruth also admired Robert Cushman. He taught constitutional law at the university. Constitutional law focuses on how a government works. Robert encouraged Ruth to go to law school. This recommendation changed her life. At the time, few women pursued legal careers. Some of Ruth's male professors did not think women belonged in their classes.

History Makers: Past and Present

Ruth and Celia

Even though she died when Ruth was a teenager, Celia Bader continued to influence her daughter. She had taught her daughter to work hard and to be kind to other people. Ruth was also inspired by her mother's love of learning. Little is known about Celia's life. She was born in New York to Jewish immigrants and enjoyed reading. Celia worked in a clothing factory after high school. Her wages helped pay for her brother's university education. Ruth admired her mother's decision to support her brother. She later told people that Celia's life would have been better if she had lived in a time when daughters were valued as much as sons.

Ruth Bader Ginsburg

Overcoming Obstacles

At Harvard, Ruth was one of nine women in a class of 500. Only two, including her, were mothers. Still, Ruth flourished. She was the first woman to ever serve on the *Harvard* **Law Review**. She later served on Columbia's law review as well. This work goes to top students.

Even though Ruth graduated at the top of her class, she had difficulty finding a job. She was interviewed by 12 law firms. None would hire a female lawyer. One of her professors asked a Supreme Court justice to employ her as a law clerk. He refused to hire a woman for that job.

The Harvard Law Review is a student-driven publication. It has been providing its readers with articles about the law since its first issue in 1887.

History Makers: Past and Present

While teaching at Rutgers University, Ruth became pregnant with her second child. Ruth knew that some employers demoted pregnant women. Others fired them. She decided to wear loose clothing to hide her pregnancy until she signed a new contract for more work at Rutgers.

Ruth's husband died of cancer in 2010. She herself was diagnosed with cancer five times. In 1999, Ruth was treated for colon cancer. In 2009, she underwent treatment for pancreatic cancer. Two cancerous growths were removed from Ruth's left lung in 2018. The following year, she was diagnosed with pancreatic cancer for a second time. In 2020, she announced that she was being treated for a cancerous **lesion** on her liver. Ruth returned to the bench each time. However, in September of that same year, Ruth died of pancreatic cancer.

In 2009, 19 days after surgery for pancreatic cancer, Ruth attended President Barack Obama's first address to a joint session of Congress.

Ruth Bader Ginsburg

Achievements and Successes

Ruth dedicated her life to human rights. As a lawyer and judge, she supported the fair treatment of all people. She advocated for people with disabilities. On the Supreme Court, Ruth defended laws that protect women's rights. She spoke against laws that took away those rights.

After accepting President Bill Clinton's nomination to the Supreme Court, Ruth went on to be confirmed by an overwhelming vote of 96–3 in the Senate.

In 1970, Ruth co-founded the first U.S. legal journal about women's rights. It is still published today. She was also the first director of the ACLU's Women's Rights Project. This project challenged laws that treated men and women differently.

In 1995, the Academy of Achievement gave Ruth its Gold Plate Award. The academy is an American non-profit organization. It introduces young people to adults who make the world a better place.

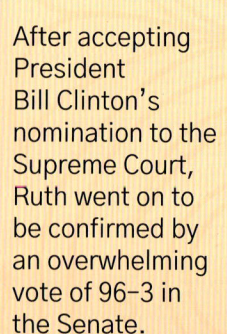

History Makers: Past and Present

More awards followed. In 2002, Ruth was inducted into the National Women's Hall of Fame, which celebrates the achievements of American women. Ruth also received the Berggruen Prize for Philosophy and Culture in 2019 for her work in equality rights. She gave the $1 million prize to charity. In 2020, the associate justice received the Lyndon B. Johnson Liberty & Justice for All Award. This award goes to people whose work supports justice and freedom.

Several books have been written about Ruth. In 2018, a feature film was released. It told the story of one of the first cases she argued before the Supreme Court.

The Liberty Medal

The Liberty Medal was given to Ruth on September 17, 2020, the day before she died. The medal honored her devotion to life and liberty for all people. It was presented by Philadelphia's National Constitution Center (NCC). The award was announced on August 26, 2020. That day was the 100th anniversary of the 19th Amendment, which gave women in the United States the right to vote.

Ruth Bader Ginsburg

Write a Biography

A person's life story can be the subject of a book. This kind of book is called a biography. Biographies describe the lives of remarkable people, such as those who have achieved great success or taken important actions to help others. These people may be alive today, or they may have lived many years ago. Reading a biography can help you learn more about a remarkable person.

At school, you might be asked to write a biography. First, decide who you want to write about. You can choose a Supreme Court Justice, such as Ruth Bader Ginsburg, or any other person. Then, find out if your library has any resources about this person. Learn as much as you can about him or her. Write down the key events in this person's life. What was this person's childhood like? What has he or she accomplished? What are his or her goals? What makes this person special or unusual?

A concept web is a useful research tool. Read the questions in the following concept web. Answer the questions in your notebook. Your answers will help you write a biography.

Writing a Biography

Adulthood
- Where does this individual currently reside?
- Does he or she have a family?

Childhood
- Where and when was this person born?
- Describe his or her parents, siblings, and friends.
- Did this person grow up in unusual circumstances?

Your Opinion
- What did you learn from your research?
- Would you suggest these resources to others?
- Was anything missing from these resources?

Work and Preparation
- What was this person's education?
- What was his or her work experience?
- How does this person work? What is or was the process he or she uses or used?

Main Accomplishments
- What is this person's life's work?
- Has he or she received awards or recognition for accomplishments?
- How have this person's accomplishments served others?

Help and Obstacles
- Did this individual have a positive attitude?
- Did he or she receive help from others?
- Did this person have a mentor?
- Did this person face any hardships? If so, how were the hardships overcome?

Ruth Bader Ginsburg

Ruth Bader Ginsburg Timeline

Ruth Bader Ginsburg Events		World Events
Joan Ruth Bader is born on March 15 in Brooklyn, New York.	**1933**	Adolf Hitler is appointed leader of Germany.
Ruth graduates from Columbia Law School.	**1959**	Fidel Castro becomes prime minister of Cuba.
Rutgers University School of Law hires Ruth as a professor.	**1963**	U.S. President John F. Kennedy is **assassinated** in Dallas, Texas.
As a lawyer for the ACLU, Ruth makes history by winning a Supreme Court case against gender discrimination.	**1971**	Women in Switzerland get the right to vote in federal elections.
Ruth is sworn in as associate justice of the U.S. Supreme Court.	**1993**	Kim Campbell becomes the first female prime minister of Canada.
Ruth supports a Supreme Court decision to strike down a rule that banned women from attending the Virginia Military Institute.	**1996**	South Africa adopts a new constitution that guarantees equal rights for all citizens.
On September 18, Ruth dies of cancer in Washington, DC.	**2020**	A new virus causes a global **pandemic**. Scientists believe the pandemic might have killed more than 3 million people in this year alone.

History Makers: Past and Present

Key Words

assassinated: killed in a surprise attack for political or religious reasons

associate justice: a judge on the Supreme Court who is not the chief judge

borough: a town, or a district within a large town, that has its own government

Constitution: the document that details the rights and responsibilities of a country's citizens under the law

discriminated: treated someone differently based on a prejudice or bias

feminist: a person who supports women as equal to men

furrier: a person who prepares or deals in furs

general counsel: the main lawyer of an organization or business

Great Depression: a period of time that began in 1929 and included worldwide economic problems

jabots: scarf-like pieces of cloth or lace that hang in the center front of a dress or blouse

jurist: an expert in or writer on law

law review: a journal with articles that focus on legal issues

lesion: an area of abnormal body tissue

pandemic: the worldwide spread of a new disease or illness

prosecutor: a lawyer who presents the case against a person in court

scholarship: a grant or payment that supports a student's education

solicitor general: an officer of the law who supports the attorney general, or chief law officer

tenure: job protection given after a trial period

valedictorian: a student, typically with the highest marks, who gives a speech at a class's graduation ceremony

Index

American Civil Liberties Union (ACLU) 10, 18, 22
awards 18, 19, 21

Bader, Celia 6, 8, 11, 15
Bader, Nathan 6
Brooklyn, New York 6, 8, 22

cancer 8, 9, 17, 22
Carter, Jimmy 10
Clinton, Bill 18
Columbia Law School 9, 10, 16, 22
Coney Barrett, Amy 13
Cornell University 8, 14
Cushman, Robert 14

Day O'Connor, Sandra 13

Ginsburg, Martin 8, 9, 17

Harvard Law School 8, 9, 13, 16

Kagan, Elena 13

Liberty Medal 19

Nabokov, Vladimir 14

Obama, Barack 17

Rutgers University 10, 17, 22

Sotomayor, Sonia 13
Supreme Court 5, 10, 12, 13, 16, 18, 19, 20, 22

women's rights 10, 18

Ruth Bader Ginsburg 23

AV2 Get the best of both worlds.

AV2 bridges the gap between print and digital.

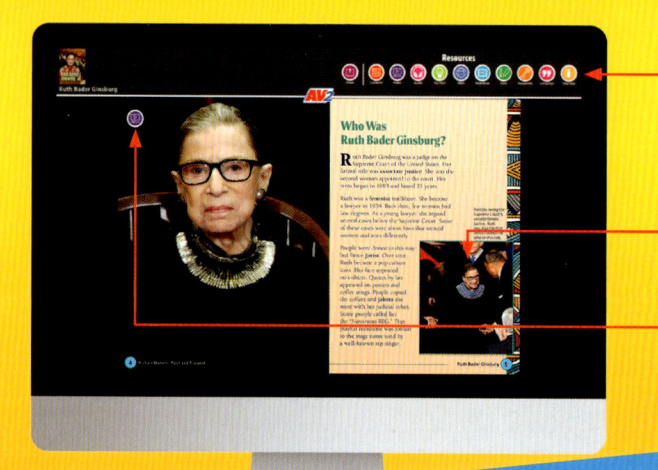

The expandable resources toolbar enables quick access to content including **videos**, **audio**, **activities**, **weblinks**, **slideshows**, **quizzes**, and **key words**.

Animated videos make static images come alive.

Resource icons on each page help readers to further **explore key concepts**.

Published by Lightbox Learning Inc.
276 5th Avenue
Suite 704 #917
New York, NY 10001
Website: www.openlightbox.com

Copyright ©2023 Lightbox Learning Inc.
All rights reserved. No part of this publication may be reproduced, stored in a retrieval system, or transmitted in any form or by any means, electronic, mechanical, photocopying, recording, or otherwise, without the prior written permission of the publisher.

Library of Congress Cataloging-in-Publication Data

Names: Gregory, Joy, author.
Title: Ruth Bader Ginsburg / Joy Gregory.
Description: New York : Lightbox Learning Inc., 2022. | Series: History makers: past and present | Includes index. | Audience: Grades 4-6
Identifiers: LCCN 2022001870 (print) | LCCN 2022001871 (ebook) | ISBN 9781791146252 (library binding) | ISBN 9781791146269 (paperback) | ISBN 9781791146276
Subjects: LCSH: Ginsburg, Ruth Bader, 1933-2020--Juvenile literature. | Judges--United States--Biography--Juvenile literature. | Women judges--United States--Biography--Juvenile literature. | United States. Supreme Court--Officials and employees--Biography--Juvenile literature.
Classification: LCC KF8745.G56 G74 2022 (print) | LCC KF8745.G56 (ebook) | DDC 347.73/2634 [B]--dc23/eng/20220208
LC record available at https://lccn.loc.gov/2022001870
LC ebook record available at https://lccn.loc.gov/2022001871

Printed in Guangzhou, China
1 2 3 4 5 6 7 8 9 0 26 25 24 23 22

022022
101121

Project Coordinator: Heather Kissock
Designer: Terry Paulhus

Photo Credits
Every reasonable effort has been made to trace ownership and to obtain permission to reprint copyright material. The publisher would be pleased to have any errors or omissions brought to its attention so that they may be corrected in subsequent printings. The publisher acknowledges Alamy and Getty Images as its primary image suppliers for this title.

View new titles and product videos at www.openlightbox.com